T0207728

A
Mask
for
Every
Occasion

MY STORY (THE FIRST 24 YEARS)

Ke-Ke Kline

WESTBOW
PRESS®
A DIVISION OF THOMAS NELSON
& ZONDERVAN

WestBow Press books may be ordered through booksellers or by contacting:

WestBow Press
A Division of Thomas Nelson & Zondervan
1663 Liberty Drive
Bloomington, IN 47403
www.westbowpress.com
1 (866) 928-1240

Scripture taken from the King James Version of the Bible.

ISBN: 978-1-9736-7343-9 (sc)
ISBN: 978-1-9736-7342-2 (e)

Print information available on the last page.

WestBow Press rev. date: 10/22/2019

"The Struggles You Are In Today; Is Developing the Strength You Need For Tomorrow"

WHO WOULD HAVE thought that today would have been the day that I would really understand the meaning of this statement and why it means so much. Then finally realizing that I have lived it, and still living it. With a better understanding of the struggles and how I sustains through them. Knowing that all this time God is and will always be my "Strong Tower" and has prepared me for such a time as this, so I give Him all Glory, Honor, and Praise.

To my children if I had the chance to say anything to any of you it will be that you all have shaped and taught me how to love without conditions, allowing me to make mistakes and still loving me through all my flaws and mishaps, then giving me the world's greatest gifts,(your children and your extended families).

Mom and dad for giving me life, the lessons learned, and watching you both smile in my most difficult times, and teaching me how not to wear my feelings or problems on my sleeves for the world to see.

My sisters and brothers, all of you have helped me in your own special ways, and it is and has been appreciated. The many advise; some that helped in my growth as a woman, a mother and grandmother, a wife and a woman of God, I thank you. And for those advice that wasn't so pleasant or constructive, I've learned to love each of you for who are.

To the rest of my family members, I say; be who you are. Learn from mistakes, love one another no matter what, and never allow misunderstandings to cause anger, hatred, malice, or unforgiveness. We are "Family" the very core of God's love, His Mercy, and His Grace, and if you can learn to keep Him first in all you do, say, and hope to be, the sky is the limit. Because we serve a "LIMITLESS GOD"

REFLECTIONS: Having serious Thoughts or Consideration.

To Think, To Contemplate, To Meditate and Ponder.

My Story

THIS STORY OF my life took flight one afternoon as I was sitting in my yard about 3 years ago. In that moment, I started reflecting back on my life and so many thoughts began to flood my mind with questions as to who I am, why I am here and how I got to where I am today.

Twenty-five years ago when I was at the very end of my rope, wanting to let go and to end it all, something went off in the pit of my stomach; so it seemed. It wasn't loud or demanding, but strong and comforting, and it shook me in a way that was so indescribable. I have no words to explain, but when it spoke these words into my spirit I knew it was the voice of the Lord.

"A Mask for Every Occasion" these words has stuck with me for a large portion of my life, even when I tried to ignore it, that voice inside kept repeating itself over, and over again. Then after being prophesied to twice, from two women on opposite sides of the globe, I knew that I had to step out without fear, having no regrets, trusting that voice for guidance, and believing that my life was created with a purpose.

At a glance, many would say, I had a good life, but if they only knew the devastating things that took place in my childhood and during this journey of becoming the woman of God that I am today. Sharing details of my life has never been a thought of mine, so I hid it behind several faces and moved on. The good, the bad, and the ugly; they were all mine and I kept them all hidden inside without exposing the real me to the world.

Many time, with a lack of understanding as to why I was chosen to go through some of the experiences I did, I often assumed it was just the way my life was to be. Today, I know that all my experiences was shaped by some personal choices, and choices of others that caused the most damaging, was the actions that were inflicted by the people I loved most.

My life had become so use to the conflicts, dysfunction, and brokenness that I believed it was normal. Being battered and beaten, abused, accused, but most of all confused. All of this; just so one day I would be telling my story and how it all became my truth; with Gods wisdom, His understanding, and my faith.

"Wisdom is the principal thing; therefore get wisdom:
And with all thy getting, get understanding" Prov.4:7

Speaking about God and having a relationship with Him is two different things and I learned that the hard way and for reasons I'm so grateful that I did. I thank Him for all I went through and all that I have learned. I am still learning, but most of all, I thank Him for His indwelling spirit that keeps me grounded and planted on a sure foundation and anchored in His care and comfort for life.

My Motto: *Because He gave His Son, and His Son gave His life, I owe Him my Life.*

The Community

FROM THE BEGINNING I knew I was different, I never could figure it out, but tried to fit in any way. I felt so out of place, but did I understood that as a child? No I didn't.

I was made fun of, and often laughed at because of the color and texture of my hair. Yes my hair; because I was the only girl with sandy brown hair that looked like wool, and I hated it. Hair like wool; what a joke. It wasn't until later in life I got the real understanding of that statement.

Let me share with you who I am. Born on the 10th day of March in 1965 to one "Big Tommy" and "Tiny". The youngest of 10 siblings, 2 of whom have gone on to their place of rest.

I am a mother of 5 children, one who has also gone on to his place of rest. I am a grandmother to 18 grandchildren. Whew; sounds like a lot right? It's awesome; therefore I get to travel and I love that.

I wish I could tell you that I had a normal childhood but I didn't, it was topsie, turvy and many times upside down, so I thought that was normal, but it was far from it. Don't get me wrong, I really appreciate where I came from, but to understand me, one must go beyond what the eyes could see because it wasn't what went on on the outside, but those things that went on behind the close doors.

Being that I was the baby of the family I didn't get to do a lot of what my elder brothers and sisters did as far as working in the fields, feeding the animals and caring for the home while our parents worked. Speaking about our home, well; it had 4 rooms and 1 of them was not a bath room that was outside which was called the "Outhouse".

We used lamps, we pumped our water, (from a outdoor pump) and cooked on a wood stove. (The best food you could ask for) there was no TV, but what we had was our imagination with a whole lot of creation.

I was raised in a time where everybody in the community was your elder, and respect was number one. We played outside, we ate what was harvest by our families and others, and everything was shared within that community.

We had our differences, and as children we fought, we fell out, we got mad, but one thing we had back then that is so missing today, "The Village" were the grownups didn't get involved in any of our childhood brawls, there was no police, no courtrooms, no judge, no cursing out one another, no one went to jail, and diffidently no one got murdered.

The fear of the Lord was instilled in us and we lived everyday knowing that He was watching everything that was done and said. Yeah; the community lived by the words of God, at least that's what I saw, and not ever dear to question anything or anyone about it.

Loving and caring about the needs of others was the way we all looked at life and that was spread abroad. We did not live separated; blacks as well as whites stuck together and it never mattered. We played together, went to school together and all that mattered was keeping the community together. That was until I moved on the other side of the creek.

The Move

THE SUMMER OF 1968 my parents decided that it was time for a new home because the one we were in had been falling apart piece by piece, a patch here, and a patch there, and that became a bit too much so my father started with trying to get land divided between his brothers and himself, only asking for what was rightly his, but came up against much adversities by the name of "FAMILY".

Let me tell you this; for I have walked this road many times in my life and I'm still trying to understand family.... I'll tell of my fights later.

My father, known to all by "Big Tom" was a gentle giant, he was a soft spoken man with a big heart. You would think that a man that stood 6'4" and weighing in at 365lb solid would be intimidating right? Well; u wrong, it wasn't my dad that people stayed away from it was my mother Tiny.

Dad was a man that loved life, he believed in having a good time no matter where he was. He was stern, but fair in his dealing with us and others. His words was his bond, and when he spoke it was over, no long discussions, no arguments, he said what he had to and he was gone.

My mother, on the other hand was something else. A fireball, short and petite but lord she could set ablaze with just her words. Tiny was not a woman to take lightly. She stood at 4'11" and wore about 110 (maybe wet) that is until her later years, and when she set her mind to doing something she went hard after it. And that was the outcome of the new home and the move.

When dad was refused by his brothers for the land, sister girl went out searching and didn't stop until she had what she needed for her family. It wasn't where she wanted, but she felt she had no other choice.

If I had something to say about where we were moving, I would have not chosen to be there either because of the many ghostly stories that was told about that side. Some of them I believed while others I lived to see and witness for myself, but to a 7 year old, that was certainly a scary place to be. That was until I got older to understand that all those stories about "Bad Blood" between the two sides was all exaggerated stories.

The house was finished, but the move was not so enthusiastic for any of us, my brothers and I that is, not because we wasn't going to see our friends and the people we had grown to know, but because it was unknown territories and uncomfortable.

In October of 1969 that 3rd Saturday we moved in, didn't have much so that took only about 30 to 40 minutes and it was all done. The following Saturday the house was dedicated to the Lord, one of the many traditions of living in the South. Everything was dedicated; babies, cars, homes, and especially the harvest for that year and the animals that kept food on the tables. All the things that the people worked hard to acquire, and as the saying goes "If it wasn't for the Grace of God" we heard that a lot.

> *"But by the Grace of God I am what I am, and His Grace to me was not without effect. No, I worked harder than all of them-yet not I, but the Grace of God that was with me" (1 Cor 15:10)*

When it all was over and we settled in, it felt like heaven to have running water, electricity, a bathroom, and I had my own bedroom Wow! That was so exciting. My brothers on the other hand had to share room but with separated beds and I believed they loved that.

Life changed for all of us, mom and dad both got better paying jobs, but was still riding with others because we didn't have a vehicle at that time but got one later on, so it was hard getting around especially when it rained.

There wasn't a road for us to get in and out to the main road, only a foot path, but it wasn't long after that, that dad made a trip to the county officials, made some noise and soon after that, it could have been a little longer, but I do remember coming home from school one day and all kind of work was being done, and we got that road; which is named after my father till this day. So proud of my father.

> *Just for thoughts:*
> *"Your Future is Created by what you do Today*
> *Not Tomorrow"*

During that same year we had an addition to our home. A baby, not my parents but a grandson, which is my nephew, so now I'm asking myself; where did this baby come from and whom it belongs? Well; after a while we got the story of why he was there and to whom he belonged.

My second eldest sister, whom I only knew from hearing about her through conversations. Had left right after graduation, which was years before I was able to know her.

My older brothers were still at home, so they shared their room with this stranger whom we all grew to love. To me; it was not fair to them, but I understood having to share your space with other family members because it happened to me about 5 years later.

He was no longer a stranger any more, he was our 1st nephew and I got to show him off that is; after I stopped being upset which I did a lot growing up because I was a spoiled brat, and you can thank dad for that.

Starangers In The House

NOW IT'S 1975 and I am 13 years old, just started playing softball and carrying around my nephew wasn't fun anymore, so he stayed home with mom because now both brothers had graduate and joined the Army. {Followed in dad's footstep: World War II Veteran}

Later at the ending of that summer mom went to New York for two weeks to visit, when she returned I felt that something was going on, because when your parents went into the room and close the doors, "need not to say anymore". Some will understand why I said this, and some won't, but if you were raised like me, oh you knew what it meant.

The one thing that never happen in front of children, no discussions of any kind, and we were not permitted to be in the same room with the grownups unless it's family time (only if it was like that today).

A few months later we were told that visitors were coming, now I'm thinking "oh man" I have to share my room with someone I don't know, now I was not feeling that; (here comes that brat again). Well she came but was not alone, she had a little girl cute, but I just didn't want them there not even for a little while. How selfish of me!!!

One week and the visit was over. Two came but only one left, then it hit me; this was what that private discussion was all about and now it's my turn to share my space and again I was not a happy camper, but soon adjusted that attitude and all was forgotten.

Now Christmas was right around the corner and I was on my best behavior because I was expecting something big being that this was my first Christmas being a teenage, and this was the only thing that was more exciting to me than softball.

Being good really paid off, I got a bicycle, not only was I the first girl, but the only one. For me that was a blast, but for the other kids in the neighborhood I was no longer on their playlist. I became the enemy so now I'm really feeling what I had been told about them all along.

The name calling and being bullied was awful, and to make it worst they would start fights and I was not a fighter, not then and surely not now. I had never experience such terrible behavior in all of my 13 years so I left them alone and went back to what was comfortable, me being me, by myself.

> *"The circumstances of life, the events of life, and the people around me in life, do not make me the way I am, but reveal the way I am"*
> *(Dr. Sam Peeples)*

The same year, three major events took place in my life. One, I turned 14 so I no longer had to take my niece and nephew with me as much because they were growing up also and found other kids their age to play with, beside my eldest sister and her family had moved back and was right next door so the kids all played together which was good, so now I had more freedom, with a little longer curfew on the weekends because of softball games being played out of town.

The second, my childhood/early teen life as I knew it changed without my permission, because of the action taken towards me, I was violated in the worst way one could imagine, and my innocent was taken in the very moment, without a simple thought of what that did to me. And on that evening I wish I had been strangled to death because a part of me died.

> **"RAPE" by definition as having sexual intercourse, or any other form of sexual penetration that is carried out without that person's consent, committed by a perpetrator against a victim.**

We often hear about rape, because it's happening worldwide now and it's no longer covered up or hidden. It's happening to our young, the middle age, our elderly, our boys and girls, men and women. It's happening in our homes, our schools, our dome rooms, our jails, and especially in our churches.

This act of violence tears a way the very fiber of our being, leaving us with questions with no answers. It rips holds in our self-image, our self-worth, and without ever understanding the Why's. Like why me and Why did this happen, what did I do, how could I have stopped this from happening. Then in the back of our minds we wonder if the person(s) that is acting out this behavior understands how brutal his/her actions are.

This is a horrendous crime and the fear that leave one to live out the horror of it all, it extremely vicious, it's deliberated, and cold-blooded. The fear of being told to keep our silence, never to have any discussion, and the one that gets me fired up the most "what happens in this house stays in this house" Are you kidding' me….

I went home and waited for dad to come in, and as soon as he did I told him what happened, where it took place, and all the threats that was made. I don't know exactly what went on in that home that evening but from the sound of it, I knew it wasn't good, and for the first time in my 14 years I heard my father raised his voice and to me it sound like thunder, then it was all done and over. That incident was never spoken of ever again, but I thought about it often.

The memories of it all caused an aching inside, and for years I carried the shame, the regrets, and very fearful. I had lost myself within myself and became someone I didn't know anymore. Just the thought of who I had allowed myself to become scared me for a time because of all the anger, the resentful, I plotted revengeful, and with all that came, bitterness and hatred.

Now the third; just when I had tuck away all those feeling and things were seemingly starting to look good, the bottom of the tub fell out and once again my life was turned upside down, and inside out. And from that day when I heard those words that came out of my mother's mouth but not believing what was being said, I once again was faced with the most devastating news that ripped a hold so deep in my heart and nothing seemed right anymore. And today, that scar of losing someone I love so much the hurt and pain of that awful, and dreadful, evening will always be there in my secret place where I have hidden so many untold memories. That is until now

Just For Thoughts:
I have learned not to compare my life to anyone else, because God's plan for me is "Masterfully Unique"

Lost Without Hope

MAY 8, 1977 began as any other day, I got up first, then I got my niece and nephew up, got ready for school but then I realized mom and dad both were still at home, so I didn't think nothing of it at first; just thought they took off to handle some business. Then dad said to me "your mom is going with me to the doctor's office so you will need to come home after school, and make sure you get those children off the bus, and know what you are to do when we're not here".

We went on to school, came home as usual did our homework and what little afterschool chores we had were done, we all washed up and got ready for bed. I stayed up to wait on them to return home. It was now 8:30 pm I heard the car door slammed and I thought I heard other people talking, so I ran to the door, but it was only mom.

Here we go again "two left; but only one came back" now that was strange, so I asked mom "where was dad" and she said "dad was in the hospital" Why? I asked; he fell just as he got there to see his doctor and no one found him until 7:00 this evening, when a nurse coming on for her shift, saw him laying by the car and called for help.

Again I asked "where were you? She said "on my way home because he had to have some test done and he told me to come home and he'll call later when he was finish" but he never got a chance to see the doctor, nor did he make the call as promised.

Now I'm confused, because mom then called my sister in law to come over and asked her to stay with us while she goes back to the hospital. About 30 minutes after she got ready to leave the house the phone rang, it was the hospital calling to let her know she needed to come right away. Mom, my sister, and her husband all left.

The kids were sleeping but I could not sleep, I sat in my bed waiting, and waited, and waited, then I heard them coming into the house and the first thing I heard mom said was "where is Keke"? My sister in law said "she's in bed, but I was in the kitchen then mom turn and looked me straight in my eyes, and I asked "Where is my daddy? And she said "Ke-Ke, your daddy's not coming home he died just as I got to the hospital. My response to her was that of anger and disbelief and I said to her "do you hate me that much that you would tell me my daddy's dead"?

Don't remember what took place after that, except me running into my room and into the closet, covered myself with the clothing and began to cry. Don't know if I fell asleep or not but when the morning came I remembered coming out because I heard my sister calling me to come and get something to eat and to hang out with the other kids, that was a NO! NO!

Broken hearted and crush; yep that's me, that was who I became that evening and thereafter because I wasn't the same, even when I thought I was healed, I was still that broken little girl who had lost her only hero.

"The Lord is near the Brokenhearted and Saves The Crushed in Spirit" Psalm 34:7

When I finally came out people was everywhere, everybody trying to hug me and telling me it was going to be alright. Oh really; I just stood there staring around the room and asking myself why are these people here? I went outside, climbed up a tree and stayed there for the rest of that evening. I didn't eat, didn't play, and did not speak to anyone, I just wanted to be left alone, then; as I was sitting there in that tree I remembered what I had wrote on the closet wall the night before "I WISH I WAS DEAD".

I felt as if I had no one at that moment, and from that day until 1980, those walls held all of my intimate feelings. My secret thoughts, my future endeavors, my pain, my anger, my fears, my anger towards my mom, God, and the doctors, I just hated them all, and that closet became my safe haven that no one knew about, and I never said anything about it, because I felt no one cared enough to ask me how I felt or how I was doing.

The next day my others sisters came home along with one brother, and many other family member but I never saw my baby brother, and no one said anything until later the following week after learning that he was in the fields and by the time his commander got word his company had left to go elsewhere, then finally he got the messages and flew home.

The morning of the funeral, I remember my brother sitting at the dining room table while everyone else was getting ready or just keeping themselves busy I walked into the kitchen and hearing "A Change Is Gonne Come" by Sam Cooke playing on the radio in the background and I watched my brother, my mentor, my best friend, broke down like a baby, and as I stood there I felt like pieces of me being ripped away. That hurt more than hearing mom say "Dad had died."

He looked up and called me over to him and he held me so tight, then said to me "I will always be here for you no matter what" and he has not broken that promise yet.

The family got through those long and sad days that is until everyone had gone back to their own lives. Both sisters went back to New York, brother 1 went back to Texas, and the one I needed to stay, went on back to Germany where he resides today. But as for me, I had no one, and I had to grow up and fast.

A CHILD; IN ADULT SHOES
ADULT: **A Male or Female that have reached Maturity, No longer young, having reached the age of being fully grown.**

This is not describing me for sure. I was just a teenager carrying the weight of an adult and at this very point my life spun out of control. But I read in God's word "That the TRUTH will make you FREE: and whom the SON set free is FREE INDEED" (not my strongest point) also I've learned that the truth will do one or two things; it will make you, or break you, and in choosing the truth over continuing to lie to myself, being real, and not ashamed of the demands and punishing treatment made by others. Was my truth.

Living but having others to make choices and decisions as they saw it was my life from that point on because everybody else knew what was best for me so it seemed.

Right now as I am writing, I can truly say "I LOVE MY MOTHER" but it took many years and a whole lot of prayer to get me to say those words and when I say it took years, trust me this did not happened overnight, and I owe it all to the awesome and mighty God I serve, that has taught me how to forgive, and in trusting Him; I've learned how to live and love beyond the physical hurt and the emotional pain.

Remember when I said earlier that mom was the tower of strength that held our family together? Well; that she was, but when dad died I watched that pillar of strength crumbled.

Alcoholism; was another subject that was never spoken of, in or out of the house, we saw it, and the effects of it, but no one understood it. I knew something was wrong but I couldn't tell anyone. It wasn't until long after leaving home and looking into it that I learned it is a disease, and I wanted to learn all I could about it, so I could have answers for anyone that was connected to me by blood or not, struggling with that horrible disease.

I grew up fast having to care for mom, my niece, nephew, help with homework, and keeping the house, because our home had fell apart so I did whatever it took to carry on.

Mom and I argued about everything, and her words were not good, it cut deep, she was quick and very sharp and it cut to the very fiber of who I was becoming. When I didn't want to deal with her I would hang outside until she went to bed. I learned how to shut her out quickly because I didn't want to hear anything anymore. There were times I would look right at her, seeing her lips moving, but didn't hear a word.

Teaching myself how to go within myself was my escape route from the cursing, name calling, and the beating. I don't know who came up with this phrase "Sticks and Stones may break your bones;

but Words will never hurt you" well I have this to say; that is one of the GREATEST LIE ever told because words hurts and it stick with you forever, especially if there is no proper healing.

He heals the brokenhearted and binds up their wounds.
(Psalm 107:20)

By my sixteenth birthday something else took place without my permission thinking it was alright because those were the words whispered into my ear, and I was just that naive to believe it and that no one would find out. Well low and, behold three months had past and I knew something was wrong because my monthly friend didn't show up. I was so afraid not knowing what to do, or where to go, surely I couldn't go to mom, neither any of my teachers, because they would have went straight to her anyway.

So here I am having nowhere to go and no one to turn too, and to make it worst; one afternoon while mom and I was out shopping, we ran into one of her older friends that looked at me, then back at mom and said "you better take that child to the doctor cuz' she is pregnant, see how glassy them eyes are" once again I wanted to disappear because I knew what the outcome was going to be.

Have you ever been slapped so hard it feels as if your face has fallen off? Not only that but being choked until you feel yourself passing out? Then having to make yourself throw up just so you could survive? Well let me help you out just in case you or someone you know is/have been in this situation.

Its's not pretty it's not funny, nor is it something to joke about. I had this happen to me on many occasions without any regards to my feelings, then to have harsh words yelled in your face all the while fighting to be let go so you could breathe.

Survival is/was my only option, then as well as now because God has placed a fighting spirit that will make other wonder how I made it to where I am today. Never should we be afraid to fight for our lives, it's a gift firm God and no one has the right to make it miserable or uncomfortable. And we are to live this life as any other person(s) do, with all of our flaws, our mistakes, our past, and our fears, looking forward to our future as God has planned. So what: I messed up.

"Not that which goeth into the mouth defileth a man: but that which cometh out of the mouth, this defileth a man." Matt 15:11

Again I was told where I should have been, where I needed to go, and what I needed to do, as if I wasn't already feeling like trash, that conversation went on for about an hour or so, that is until I retrieved to my room.

Two days later I came home early from school because I wasn't feeling well, now why did I do that.

As a mother I know I have said some things and done some things but when I look at my children and watch them grow up into who they are today it makes me wonder how could anyone ever allow themselves to say hurting words, as to harm them in any way, how is it possible to do these things to someone you love. Well I have this as an answer and had to figure this out the hard way.

When we are young, we expect the grownups in our lives to act as such (grownups). Not realizing that they are human and have many things going on in their lives also. We look at our parents as our gods because it's through them we learn how to love, to care, they are our strength, our safety nets, and so much more, and when this is all disrupted and everything we thought of them has been replaced with harmful words and terrifying acts, it leave us wondering what went wrong?

The teenager that I was, had become confused, unclear, and puzzled because I no longer was able to identify with this behavior and that alone led me into making some stupid decision.

"His grace keeps working, even in my pain and brokenness"

Illusion: A distortion of the senses, revealing how the brain normally organizes and interprets reality.

Object Of Desire: Love Or In Lust

THE OBJECT OF my affection; what a joke that turned out to be. If I knew then what I know now about the difference between love and lust and how these two words takes on a whole new meaning when your eyes become open. Only God knows.

Well here it is two years later, now eighteen with 2 children and 1 on the way. Still confused, hurt, ashamed, a high school dropout, living on Welfare, and in the family home. Wanting so much to believe that love was possible even for me, but then I learned, that in order to have another person's love, the way I deserved it, I had to first love myself.

I may have been deceived, but I got the best of the best, and have no regrets (at least not now), but I did when I was left to carry the load all alone.

The girls, my girls, and Gods young ladies are all grown up and living their own lives. They all have children, and husbands, homes, and careers, so you know I am one proud mother. Especially; when they were label as the kids that weren't going to be anything, weren't going anywhere, and wasn't going to have anything but a house full of children just as I did. Yeap; that was the word on the streets, (like mother, like daughter(s). News flash! The devil is a Liar.

When God has His hands in the mist of one's life, it doesn't matter how many times you mess up, He honors His promises even when we don't honor ours.

I believed somewhere in the back of my mind I knew it all the time that things wasn't going to work out, but yet I tried, having high hopes that I was wrong about what I was feeling. The main ingredient was missing (LOVE), and it took me three kids later to realize that I was in love with the idea of what I thought was love when all the time it was just pure lust. It was all an illusion that wasn't going anywhere, but my heart was saying something else.

I wanted so much to leave from where I was, and I did after many years of struggling to do what was right by my children, God allowing me to go back to school, and getting my diploma, and still before leaving to get away from all the drama, I ended up living in a home for unwed mothers, then moving back again to the same old habits.

Working like a slave to make ends meet and then to top it off, having to fight for wanting to take on my own responsibilities as a mother.

My first pregnancy was good, for the first time in my life I weight more the 95lbs. As the pregnancy continued I gained lots of weight and by the time of delivery I wore a whopping 172lbs and that was no fun in middle of the summer. In the very last week of the pregnancy I went out with some friends, and dance myself right into the hospital, at 11:40pm here comes my first bundle of joy weighting in at 7lbs/6oz.

This was a whole new world for me because she wasn't just any baby, she was my baby, and that became so emotional. She was a happy baby that loved to eat, never cried much and that was great, because I had to get up for school in the mornings and just preparing for that was a task by itself.

My eldest sister had left to raise her family in the city, then the third sister felt it was time to leave also because there was no getting along at home either, it had just gotten to where she couldn't take the verbal abuse anymore so once again; I was left alone.

I had no idea about what to do or where to start but I was determined to do my best.

The greatest hardship in those earlier days was that I had no money to purchase pampers so they wore cloth diapers which required washing every day, and I didn't enjoy doing that at all. For one; it had to be hand washed out of a foot tub because I was not allowed to wash them in the washing machine. Secondly; they had to be bleach white before they were put on the line, and if it wasn't they were removed and I had to do them all over again.

My niece and nephew helped out when I had other chores along with checking their homework, and having my own homework done, whereas all of this had to be done by 7:30pm so that dinner and bathing were done and us being (not getting ready) in the bed by 9:00pm.

Well; time past and I went about doing all that I was used to doing nothing change, except me getting knocked up again. I didn't tell anyone because there was nothing to tell, neither was there any physical change in my body and that's how I concealed it for the seven month except for the fact that I was also in denial, that is before I really got myself into trouble.

On this particular Saturday I went on the farm as usual, I think we were picking Bell Peppers at that time, and yes; I worked on the farm during my pregnancy, but this day I had begun to feel bad so I left and went home but when I got there things was not looking good, so I went over to the kids aunts home and still said nothing to anyone.

I just sat there; that is until I was hit accidently on my foot and within seconds, I lost it, and that turned into an altercation. Lord what was I thinking?

I didn't think, I just reacted out of anger because I knew that was how I had learned to behave for protection. When it was all over I went home and laid down just to get up to go to the bathroom and saw I was bleeding and water was all over the floor that's when I knew I was in labor and didn't know what to do but to call his sister and she got me to the hospital just in time to go straight to the delivery room.

In minutes my second child was born and she was in trouble, and when I say trouble, it was scary; she was born premature at seven month weighting only 1lb/3oz so she had to be taken into the pre-natal care unit quickly. I did not see her, I could not hold her, all I was left with was a sinking hold in my stomach full of fear that she was not going to live, and even more afraid of what God was going to do to me for not telling the truth and hiding this child.

Just for thoughts
"A fool gives full vent to his anger, but a wise man keeps himself under control". (Prov 29: 91)

Yes I was that fool. But God; I finall left the hospital after a week or so but without my child. She was airlifted to another medical center where the prenatal clinic was more equipped in handling babies in her condition (early delivery and low birth weight).

After about a month I was able to visit, she had gained 1lb but her immune system was still weak so I still wasn't able to whole her yet. Looking at her through that incubator was very emotional, she had so many different tubes and needles connected to her little legs, and being fed through her head blew me away, but with all that going on I didn't notice that she was off the resprirator and breathing on her own. What a blessing to see this miracle from the hands of God.

Two weeks later, while in class I was informed I had an emergency call from the hospital saying I needed to come up as soon as possible. Nervous and shaking out of my skin for not knowing what to expect, or the urgency for my visit.

I lost all sense of concentration and going to class was out of the question. At the end of that week I made the decision to quit school so that all of my energy could be focusing on the baby.

That Friday I spoke to mom about my decision and she said to me "when you get to that hospital, I want you to check that baby out and bring her home because those doctors don't know anything about us". That statement alone left me not knowing what to do at this point.

While waiting on the clinic bus and wondering what happens now (when I arriving at the clinic), so I rushed up to the room to see what was going on, and to my surprise when I walked in the nurse was holding her and told me to get washed up and ready to hold her for the first time, you could not imagine all the emotions I felt at that moment.

When I got her, I held her close to my chest so that she could feel my heartbeat and even with her being wrap so tight I could see her tiny, little, perfect face, and in my heart I was screaming "Thank you Lord" so loud; that I made a promise to God that I would do all I Could to live a better life, without lying and hiding behind the faces, so that others could not hurt or take advantage of me again.

> *"Wash me thoroughly from mine iniquity, and cleanse*
> *me from my sin. For I acknowledge my transgressions;*
> *and my sin is ever before me" (Psalm 51:2-3)*

Two month had pass since that awesome visit, she gained another 1lb and a half so I did what I was told to do and had her discharged to go home.

As I was finishing up the paperwork, her doctor walked over to me and spoke these words "against my better judgement, if you remove her out of our care she may or may not survive no longer then about 2 weeks at the most" in shock and disbelief I looked at her and said "you don't know the doctor I do" and I left, but those words continue to song off in my head and what was an hour ride seemed like it took forever.

Finally; when I arrived at home mom met me at the door and without a word she took the baby and went straight to the kitchen where she had this large pot of girts, a large piece of cheese cloth, and some torn piece of sheet laying on the counter top. Again; I'm wondering, what's going on, with eyes blaring, watching my mom as she took some of starch from the top of the grits, and poured it onto the cheese cloth, to cool down, she took the baby unwrapped her, and slowly placed her unto the cloth, she then took some of the starch and rubbed it onto her skin, then wrapped her in it tightly just as she was when I brought her home.

I was told not to remove her from that wrap for the next two month, the only thing I was to do, was to wash her face with warm milk every other day. And I did that for the entire two month without questions, even when I wanted to know the purpose of it all I knew not to ask but just to do what was told of me to do.

At the end of the two month it was amazing to finally see my baby being able to hold her head up, her little legs were kicking, and she was now able to digest baby cereal. Wow! Yet another miracle, then mom told me to go give her a bath in warm milk and let God do what only He can do.

I think I mention this before about mom, she had her ways but the one thing I admired about that small woman was that she had some awesome faith and it was that faith that kept me going, in spite of our relationship, she was a praying woman.

After witnessing this amazing act of God through my mom, and knowing the condition my child was in, to where she is today still amaze me. Having to watch her grow up to be such a strong young woman after being told she would not have survive because I decided once again, to follow the instructions of another. But God has proven that with Him, nothing is impossible.

The Promise

WHEN YOU ARE afraid and feel as if there is no hope because you can't see nothing but fear and dismay, you will do whatever it takes to find what you need and that is exactly what I did and promised God from that day because "He" allowed my child to live, I would serve Him for the rest of my life.

Did I keep that promise? Yes I did, did I fall? Yes I did, over and over and over again, but I never forgot the promise and with my whole heart I tried to do what was right but again I messed up by getting pregnant for the third time. Well; that didn't turn out the way it was planned, and for the third and final time that piece of my heart was split beyond repair, so I thought.

I was devastated, and felt alone, and having to deal with all of the things that was going on in my head knowing others were talking about the situation, I felt as if I was the joker in the deck, so I packed up and went to a home for unwed mothers.

I was a wreak when I got to the home, I couldn't stop crying, I was "ANGRY" no that's not the truth I was FURIOUS and the only way I could deal with it all was to do what I've always done, shut down, and shut myself out from the world and the people around me for a moment to think.

Spending those days alone gave me lots of time to think about what and where my life had gone so fast without realizing that a large portion of it had pass me by, and now all that's left is to figure out how I was to do what was best for those children.

With all that was going on with me, one day I looked up and realized I had really begun to enjoy being there and with other young ladies that was in the same predicament as myself. We all had some things going on in our lives that lead us there, to a place of safety, with no one to judge you, no one controlling you, and to learn we all had a voice in making the best decision concerning us and the child we were carrying.

A place where we all shared one common denomination, to get our lives back on track and to move forward without any regrets.

During my time at the home many thoughts came to mind, but the one that I knew for sure was that I had to get off of that fantasy Island I was on and put an end to the madness.

About 2 month into my stay, I received a call and the voice on the other end asking "have I made a decision about where do we go from here"? And for a brief moment I wanted to saying "I think we could work it out for the sake of the children" but just as quick as that thought surface, I began to think about all of what I had already went through and all the anger I felt, I was able to keep my composure and said; "As far as (we) go there is no we, but as for these girls you will always have the right to be in their lives, but even that choice is up to you.

For the first time I made a decision and choice that I no longer wanted to be in that relationship any longer. That day I grew up, made a difficult decision, that was beneficial for us, my babies and me.

On October 5, 1984 at 1:20pm I went into labor. When we arrived at the hospital the administrator and me, the doctor and staff were waiting on us. I was then taken to another area separated from the main entrance that was only for us, the young ladies that came in from the home. The rooms were beautiful and very comfortable having everything needed for delivery (which didn't take long).

During the delivery there were some problems because the IUD that was inserted after the second delivery had tangled itself in my umbilical cord which caused labored breathing and a faint heartbeat, so I had to undergo minor surgery to have it remove, to save her life. All went well and I had another beautiful girl weighting in at 6lb 7oz. OH MY GOODNESS!!! that's all I could say at that moment because

I was so tired and I believed I fell asleep right away, then waking up to the cries of my third and beautiful baby.

> *Just for thoughts:*
> *Someday everything will make perfect sense. So, for now, laugh at the confusion, smile through the tears and keep reminding yourself that everything happens for a reason.*

One month after giving birth, it was time for me to go home (back to the drama) just in time for a mini war. Now let me ask this question; why is it that when you give people an inch they take it upon themselves to take a mile?

When I left, the care of the children was in trusted to be cared for by someone I trusted; believing that when I returned their needs and concerns would be my responsibility, but that was far from what it turned out to be.

So I let my guards down total controlled, without any regards as to what I had to say or do. It was that way or hit the highway; Oh really; never again was I going to allow anyone to have that much power over me. I was back and ready to take on the responsibility of raising those children that God entrusted to me.

I couldn't understand the reason for the behavior then, but as I got older and wiser it became clearer as the years went on and me learning how to take a different approached to understanding ones behavior. I really appreciative for given all that had taken place in my absence and very grateful for all the help when I needed it the most.

> *"And to esteem them very highly in love for their work's sake. And be at peace among yourselves".*
> *(1Thess 5:3)*

I never doubted that it was going to be hard, but I also knew that it all would have worked out for the best because of the promise and believing God was going to see me through every area and aspect of my life. I also knew that He was the only source I could trust for the children needs and our well-being.

But with each decision I made it was never good or right enough. I was questioned, criticized, put down and talked about and yes; it hurt but I did not allow that to stop me from doing what I thought was best even with that, it always led to an argument and that drove me crazy.

Those arguments lead me to take some drastic measures, and at that time, it was my way to escape from it all and moved on. I not only regressed within myself, but other sides (two to be exact) of me would surface each time without knowing how to control what was happening or not even knowing who these other person(s) where.

I was lost and didn't know why or when I was drawn into all this darkness. So now I'm beginning to question my sanity or insanity which ever it was, but it wasn't me, not the young lady that promised to live a life dedicated to the Lord for all the wonderful blessing that was poured out over the course of her jacked up, torn up, from the floor up life. Yes; it was me; with my save, sanctified, baptized, walking with the Lord, (so I thought) and making promises that I didn't keep myself.

It was me, drawn into a place where the very thought of who I had become was frightening, but real. I had so much rage surprised inside and there wasn't any way of dealing with it all so I allowed my good to be taken over by evil. The evil thoughts, the evil words, the evil actions, and the evil reactions, that's who I was. Divided in three; Ke-Ke, Jennifer, and Michelle, but which one was the real me. Oh those mask.

Jennifer, was the part of me that did not care about anything or anyone. If she was hurt, she was determined to hurt you back at any cost, because of rage, anger, bitterness, that was kept in a place behind a mask, hiding from the people that had inflicted pain thought out my life. And she wanted revenge, and every time I came under attack, she came out with a vengence.

The plots and planning wasn't good for me or others around me and I knew that if I allowed Jennifer to take total control, and to do what she wanted to do it would have cost me my life, ending in prison, or death, and the worst; to lose my children? Well; I don't want to even think about that. But when I looked back, I'm so grateful I did take the time to really think about it.

Michelle; she was the one with a calmness of spirit, she was more receptive, and with much humility, she had a more subtle way of dealing with the disappointments, the discouragement, and the turmoil that was forced upon me, so she become my voice of reason.

Later in life I remembered being told that when I was born I was to have been given the name "Michelle" now can you say; "Look at God" for in Him; I know there is no coincidence, only destiny. (Nugget) Another tidbit I learned further in my life after discovering who I was, what I was called to be, and who God really is.

> *"For I know the plans I have for you, declares the Lord, plans to prosper you and not harm you, plans to give you hope and a future." Jeremiah 29:11*

The battle between Jennifer, Michelle and myself continued for many years. Some good, some bad, and other times it was just me doing what I did to survive, sometimes I got so lost in the two worlds that I almost forget who I was.

To make this clear, I must explain what was taking place in this part of my life. Confusing? I know; but remember it is my "TRUTH"

> *Personality Disorder: is a type of mental disorder in which you have a rigid and unhealthy pattern of thinking, functioning and behaving. A person with this disorder has trouble perceiving and relating to situations and people. Personality disorders usually begin in the teenage years or early adulthood.*

Having dual personalities wasn't a conversation or a subject that was up for discuss either. I had never heard of it until 1973 when the movie Sybil came out, and decided to watch it out of curiosity after reading what it was all about. As I watched that movie and seeing that

I was experiencing the same episode as the actress, then a light went off and at that very moment, for the safety of others and myself, I started researching "spilt personality"/"personality disorder".

This was a lot for a teenager to take in but I understood that something was not right with me, because I would be a normal teen doing what teens do and as soon as I felt that I was being attack I would become out of control especially when it came to the children. I was like a dog trapped in a corner fighting my way out.

And the very thing I was afraid of, happened.

By 1985 I had been pushed, pulled, and shoved around for so long that I blew up like never before. For some reason I was being questioned about some clothing that was folded in a box rather then it being hung up. What? (fold clothes), so here I am trying to explain why, but there was no listening only yelling, and it got louder and louder, mind you now, all of this is becoming overwhelming and the anger is setting in because I was being held down.

I don't remember running into the kitchen and getting a knife but just as quick as I raised it, I was jumped in front of, caught by my arms, got picked up and taken out of the room, pushed outside, to walk around, until I came back to myself.

When I finally calmed down, I was asked "what happened and where did I go" because no one had never seen me act so viciously before, but I couldn't explain because I had no idea of what was being said, nor did I remember the incident that was being explain.

In the heat of all that was going on I (Ke-Ke) had checked out and (Jennifer) came out in full force. With no explanation to give, my brother just kept looking at me waiting for answers and I had none.

I remember him saying; I had turned into someone else and he did not recognize me in that moment because all he saw was rage and death in my eyes.

When it all was over, we went for a walk so that we could speak alone without being interrupted by others. He wanted so bad to understand what happened, and who was this other person because it sure wasn't his sister. Of course I didn't tell him anything, because I didn't know how to explain having a personality disorder. So that too; was one of the many secrets hidden for many years.

From that day, I kept my distance from others, even living in the same house, I was left alone and life went on as if it all was normal. The girls and I continued to do whatever it took to get along. Not healthy, but we survived the dysfunction of being in the home.

> *"But he that doeth wrong shall receive for the wrong which he hath done; and there is no respect of person"*

The House That Jack Built

WHO IN THE world is Jack? We heard this line often but never an explanation as to who Jack was. Living in dysfunction; yes; we had a roof over our heads, a place to sleep when night fell, and we had food to eat, but life was hard with all the mix emotions, the disagreements, and so much covering up or should I say; the many things that was swept under the rug.

During the day I wore a smile, to hide what was really going on. Always telling a joke to laugh when all I wanted to do was cry, but to ashame, and at night I cried myself to sleep-page because it was behind closed doors, knowing that the odds was against me and not only that, but many was waiting to see me fall and fail.

My cries were so intense I suffered with migraine headaches and to get some relief I would have to make myself throw up. (Sounds familiar)

The drinking had become unbearable and I hated it more now because it wasn't just me anymore the girls was there and I didn't want them exposed to that mess knowing the affects it had on me. That was not fair to them, also they were growing up so fast and taking in everything seen and heard around them.

During the day I went to school, and at night I bus tables just to make ends meet. At this time, they were being looked after by the other grandmother and walking almost a ½ mile back and forth with them so early in the mornings, in the rain, and in the winters it was just plain awful.

So as always; I did what was necessary because the vehicle was sold by this time so I purchased a wagon, not just any wagon, but a big red wagon. One that could transport the three of them, their bags, my books, and whatever else needed for that week.

I was known as "Ke-Ke and the big red wagon" to many it seemed funny because they would see me struggling just to get to where I needed to be and they would blow their horns and kept right on going. Many times hurt, angry, and crying but I kept right on pulling, until one day I looked up and the girls were big enough to walk the distance, and soon going to school themselves.

> *"Nothing could stop God's plans for your life"*
> *(Isa 14:27)*

With all that was going on in my life I still found time to play softball. The sport I loved with a passion and it was something that no one could take away from me. Those game helped me to stay focus, and away from all the negativity. I was a great player and I felt good about myself and instead of being called out of my named; I was known as the girl with the "Golden Glove" to which I won 3 trophies along with 2 MVP's. And my babies was there every time, every place, and every game.

> *"Efforts and Courage are not enough without Purpose and Direction; for every Minute you are Angry, you lose Sixty Second of Happiness."*

A Love Lost By Casualty

FOUR YEARS HAS past now and the girls and I are getting along great even with the minor itches and glitches along the way. I started dating, and of course it felt strange and out of character because all I knew was the kids, home, and softball. That was my norm; nothing less, nothing more.

It took a while for me to get comfortable with this guy so no one knew about him until Five month later when I decided to introduce him to the girls being he told me so much about his girls (2) and his family. I knew he was big on this sort of things and the only thing he knew about me was that I was a mother to 3 girls, lived on the island, I had two brothers and three sisters. I never spoke about my mom or nothing else for that matter so most of our conversations was mainly about him.

When the day came for us to get together I was so shaken that I wanted to call and tell him not to come over again but it was to late, by the time I got the kids and myself ready he was calling to ask about the directions, and now I knew it was going to be now or never.

Well it all went great with him and the girls, then out of the blue here comes mom so I had already braced myself to be embarrassed but to my surprise she behave herself like a champ, which was a shocked to me. When she came in, I introduced them and she took it from there, and it was great, no; it was awesome and she knew just as much about him as I did.

As the summer wrapped up and the softball season came to an end things between us kept right on moving but I had just one nagging question to ask from the beginning but didn't, so I just blurt it out one day and I asked "Are you married? He looked at me and laughed, now I really felt like a fool because I had put this man in a box, (with all the others that was in my life) without even knowing his intentions about our relationship. That taught me a valuabe lesson; I will not ever judge one man actions to that of another.

We laugh about it and then he said "I'm leaving for deployment and I'll be gone for about 6-8 month and I need to know will you wait for me"? With my mouth opened wide looking silly, I said "sure I will" but are you sure this is what you want? And he answered; I've never been so sure of anything in my life except my girls. All I could say was Wow! I couldn't believe that this man really wanted me and was willing to except the whole package.

Well, about 1 week later he lifted and I waited with anticipation to hear all about what his job was and how he was doing out there in the dessert heat. But no letters came, it was 3 weeks now and I had gotten a little discouraged and then here comes his first letter; I was so excited I ran all the way from the mailbox ran in the house and went straight to my room. The letter was filled with much detail and I was so glad that he was doing well, but didn't want to be there because of all the hard training he was going through but assured me he would write more often.

The letters came as promise, I believed I was getting 3 letters a month for about 4 month then all of a sudden they stopped. 1 week turned into 1month, 1 month turned into 2 month then before you know it, 5 month had passed and still no letters, by now I'm getting worried and confused so I sat down to write him, and at that same moment mom came into my room holding a large brown envelope that was delivered.

Now I'm thinking he sent me a whole lot of pictures, but to my surprise when I opened it all the letters that I wrote him within the last 3 month had return with a note attached saying "SSgt. is no longer with the company, but you can call the number below for more information".

It took me about 2 days before I got up the nerves to dial the number, and just as I thought; it was his mother, and she give me the gut busting news that he was one of the young men that was in the bombing of their company quarters 3 month ago. I said "thank you" hung up the phone, and just sat on my bed. To hurt to cry, to numb to except what I was just told, and to shock to even think.

Once again I'm experiencing the loss of someone I cared about. Taken without any warning or explanation, just gone never to be seen or heard from again, that very thought made me sick to my stomach. Angry because this person that cared about me had been taken away by casualty.

That was my "Dessert Storm" and it lifted me emotionless for about a month or so, without ever mentioning it to the girls or anyone else, I just went on with life as usual. Jennifer, Michelle, and I kept all that anger, hurt, pain, disappointment, locked inside, hiding away from the world, without coming to terms about my feelings, just shut up; never to explain.

I thought about him for a long time after that. Wondering where we would have been, how our live would have evolved with our children? But all I had was memories of my "fireball" with a smile that lit up the skies and my heart.

> **Just for Thoughts:**
> **Don't find love, let love find you.**
> **That's why it's called falling in love,**
> **Because you don't force yourself to fall, you just**
> **fall....**

Broken But Unique

"A man is but the product of his thoughts, what he thinks he becomes"

JUST ANOTHER TRUE statement. This is the one part of my life I wish I could delete forever, but because I am a survivor it gives me pleasure to share this horror story that will last me a life time of regrets.

It is now four years after the loss Sarge. I am working and making a bit more money so now I am able to do a little more for the girls and was very proud of that accomplishment.

What is it about playing softball; that draws people to me? I must ask this question because this is how I became a victim once again, and left to figure things out and wondering where I went wrong.

Things were going good, so let my guards down.

I want to first say this about abuse. In no ways is it okay for a man to hit a woman or a woman to hit on men. I also understand that many of us get caught up in these situations and find ourselves trap because of fear. I also know that many of us allow the abuse to continue because of feeling there is no way out or nowhere to go, and if you find yourself or know of some other woman/man/child(ren) in this situation, please speak up. A life could be save.

> *Tears are prayers too, they travel to God when we can't speak.*
> *(Psalm 56:8)*

The pain, the shame, the lying, and the covering up, is not a life that anyone should have to live; male or female. We as women should never ever feel that we have to take this kind of treatment from anyone. We should always feel safe in our homes, on our jobs, or wherever we go and not having to look over our shoulders because the relationship we are in is kill or be killed.

The fear of abuse that I/we experience in my/our lives becomes a cycle when we are not taught how to break away from such behaviors. We all want to trust and believe that not all relationships is based on false hope, and sometimes I/we fail to see what is right in front of Me/us. Blinded by wanted to be love, and accepted for who we are rather than what/who we are told we are/where.

The violence of abuse we may endure and sustain from a person(s) that is/was to love and protect us, could become our worst enemy. And in most cases, this is where our lives is no longer a life, then we become the person(s) that is or will be sort after because we are then label as weak. But I do know now that this has nothing to do with being weak, nor is it a matter of weakness, it's simply because we (women) and others becomes vulnerable and become another persons prey.

I know that some will ask themselves why I choose to share these incident in detail. Whole others will proably wonder why I allowed myself to stay in a place where all things was based on threats and violence. So I say this to whomever may or may not question the reason(s) that in sharing these ordeals, I pray that some other person(s) would have the strength to get help.

I'm not looking for anyone's sympathy or pity because God has given me all that I needed to stand the test of my storms. So it's in my sharing, that it would somehow open the eyes of the abuser, and those being abused or anyone that is or have been suffering in any kind of mistreatment, to know and understand that this behavior is unacceptable. And please; by all means know there is hope, and life after the facts when we put our trust in God.

The most important of this all is knowing and believing that you can survive after any form of abuse, Weather physical, mental, verbal, emotional, psychological, or sexual, you can start anew, and began to live life according to the will of God, and allow Him to do the healing and the rebuilding of your/our lives.

If it wasn't for the goodness and grace of God, I would have crumbled under the weight of all the pain, caused by putting myself in harms way, allowing the mind manipulations, and the disconnections of self and others that was around me.

I had no idea that I could really enjoy life or that I would ever get to where I am in my healing. But when I was able to let go and allow God to carry the weight and burdens that held me captive and letting His words teach me how to forgive and move on without regrets but with a greater sense of who I am and what I was created to do. To love Him first, then to forgive myself, and continue living, loving, and respecting, who I was and becoming whom I was to be.

These incidence that I'm sharing has been seared in my mind for the rest of my life. Yes; there were many, but these were the ones that were of the most brutal acts of violence that any person(s) should have to go through, then to live it all over again after seeing it on a lifetime movie. As I sat and watched that movie, I began reliving every bit of this young lady's life, and what made it more real to me was that I could feel her pain throughout every scene and at that very moment it was as if someone had peeked into my life and made this movie.

I believed the title was **"WHEN NO ONE WOULD LISTEN"** I could be off a little with the title, but this I knew for sure; this was my story and now I will allow you to experience it with me as I did with the character portrayed in the movie.

Please don't get so caught up in who, when, why, and where, but I'm asking that you focus on the what. The anger, the rage, just the very act of causing harm to another person, then allow yourself to become this person for a minute.

The young man that played the husband was a very angry person that verbalized his anger with hateful words, while physically, and sexually abusing her. He traumatized his wife and their (3) children with his acts of violence toward her and everything she stood for. He ripped the very fiber of her womanhood away and when she sort help, no one listened. So his final fit of rage ended in her death.

Just to give some highlights of what I'm talking about; I'll share the first scene and what took place so you can understand and know where I'm coming from.

I can assume that some of us have been pulled by our collar at some point in our lives right? Now envision being thrown to the floor, with a knee in the chest and a knife to the throat. Trying so hard to yell, but the grip around the neck so tight, and can hardly breath, so her only thought is to just lay there and pray that it would end soon. But not!!!

He continue hitting her repeatedly, blood everywhere, then at the same time he's dragging her into the bathroom, throws her into the bathtub, and left her there like she was nothing. So now I believed she began to ask herself what just happened. But no one to answer; how can anyone began to figure out the WHY'S? As if that wasn't bad enough, she's sitting there wondering what do I do, or where do one go after this.

She was seven month pregnant, on medical leave from her job, because of not being able to keep anything down, and she's hemorrhaging. Yet another question that had no answers. HELP!!!

Now this is where I find myself asking these same questions and having no one to answer them nor having anyone to reach out to because I'm a shame and afraid of what the outcome might be, so I climb back into my shell and behind the mask that I had learned to wear so well, hidden with a smile but fighting a battle within.

Again, I'm in this fight with me, Myself, and I, being pulled here, there, and everywhere, (The McDonald Syndrome) that's what I call it and only if you could understand exactly what I mean, because now; I had gotten so paranoid I had begun to hear voices and seeing things that weren't there. Am I going insane or what?

I knew Jennifer, harbored hate, but this kind was with such passion, that in my mind she began to plot murder and she didn't care, she loved the thrill of plotting and planning, even when I tried so hard to get away from the thoughts of doing harm, those thoughts consumed me every moment of everyday.

Now I'm not sure, (please don't quote me) but I do believe that this is what happens when any person(s) male or female is expose to any sort of violence or put in any type of life threatening situation, as with me; my thoughts were out there and yes; it went as far as believing that any person(s) that would take these kind of actions toward another was a menace to our society and that she would be doing a great favor by eliminating the problem.

This was who I had become again. My back was against the wall and as I said earlier, when this happens my second person comes out with vengeance, and with my mind not being able to think clearly, anything at that time could have taken place because I just wanted out, and by any means necessary.

Yes I understood that (rationally), I would have to give an account for whatever actions taken, but as I said; Jennifer (irrational) didn't care one way the other, she just wanted it to end, and quickly.

Here go those masks again, just hiding away behind the faces that had become a place of safety, and comfort, my place of familiarity.

Remember now; these are my truth. All I'm asking is to think of yourself or anyone that is or have been in this place, and that you allow your mind to just go with me as I take you down my memory lane of horror, my sadness, my madness, and now my laughter; right here in the mist of my healing as I continue my journey into self-realization and God's revelation.

Now put yourself here "Reality TV" and all the stories that are taken from real life incidents, then perhaps just one day while watching, and your attention is caught by this scene. But now you're seeing yourself, or maybe your daughter, a niece, and yes; this could be your mother. And this is happening every day, all over the world and it has no color, no gender, no race, or any religious affiliations.

But what it has; is a person(s) being violently attacked, just because some other person(s) don't know how to channel their anger or how to relate to the changes that comes and goes in our everyday lives. We all have our DID days (Down In The Dump) but violence is not the answer nor is it the proper outlet.

Well anyway; the storyline went on and she stayed with her husband. But things just got worst and this time it was her ending. This time the incident took place one evening as she came out of the grocery store and slipped on a piece of paper or something slippery and almost fell. But thank God there were some older gentlemen standing right outside of the doors and one of them reached out and caught her arm and held it until she got her balance.

Now as she approached the car you could see that the husband was upset, and here she is trying to explain what just took place but before she could get a word out, she was grabbed by the back of her head and her face was being slammed into the dashboard several times, and there goes the bloody nose, mind you; all of this is taking place while in the car so where can one go when there is nowhere to go.

While at the house, he stanched her out of the car, she's thrown to the ground, kicked in the stomach, picked up and thrown onto the windshield, he then pulled her off the car and again thrown, while lying there, kicking and screaming, he's pulling her by one leg, punching her in the face, and again left to clean up her bruised body, the black eye, and her bloody nose. Can you say **OUCH!!!**

About this time, I believed she was about in the middle of her eighth month, so she was moved into a shelter for battered women. While there she began thinking about her life and why all this was taken place when all she wanted was a life with the man she loved and their children.

As I watched that movie I found myself somewhat in the same position. As the tears ran down my face and flashes of my life past through my head I knew I had to make some different choices because I didn't want what happened to this woman to become my story. Because it took that woman's death (by the hands of her husband) and how she had been ignorned many time by the police not trying to intervene at some point to help or to give her information as to how she could help herself.

But her death, and only then; that it drew attention to get someone to really make domestic violence/abuse a priority and under no circumstances should it be taken lightly.

Just knowing how easy it would or could have been me, my life ending ln death, and in that quick second of memory that movie gave me a reason to speak out.

"His Grace Keeps Working, Even In My Brokenness"

Now ask yourself this question, how can any person(s) come back from such acts of violence? How do one begun to live a normal life? How do one forgive and move on ? How can one not be filled with hate and rage after such actions?

Well; this was my decision. I refused to give up, or to give in because I had four reasons why I wanted and needed to live and not die. My children, they are now, and has always been my reason to live, so I had to find a way to be the woman/mother I was meant to be.

You can breathe now, I have learned that I can and will laugh out loud (LOL) without being laugh at. I couldn't then, because nothing about that part of my life was enjoyable nor was it pleasurable. Now; as I recall these acts, it was brutal. It was sad, and it's all so funny when you think about it, because I have survived, even when the enemy attack was to kill me, "I am a survivor" And through it all, God has given me a testimony so I could be the voice for others.

"No Weapon Form Against Me Shall Prosper"

I HAD ALL REASONS to not wanted to forgive, but I knew that when my heart is hard or has been harden, faith can't get in and there is no rest, which was all I wanted.; my peace and some rest. So in that test, I had to learn to live with my heart so open, (not an easy task) that when I heard His promises it would produce what is inside of me to come out so I could live differently within myself.

But it all comes back to this same question, how can or how is it possible for any person(s) to cause deadly harm in speech or actions upon the people or person they love.

> *For I Will restore health to you, and your wounds,*
> *I will heal says the Lord. (Jer. 10:17)*

We see and hear of this sort of things happening every day, and just as I said before; we as a society has accepted it as normal. Lives are being taken and interrupted all the time because of these kind of abuse and violence. Again; it's in our homes, in our schools, our colleges, and in our churches.

Back to the story. However; three days after leaving the shelter I went into labor, my girlfriend got me to the hospital, I was then put on bedrest, and meds, to keep me from going into full labor because I had another month and a half before the full term of the pregnancy.

It's three hours later, I'm still having contractions with servere hemorrhage, but no baby. Then to top that off; the nurse comes in and says I have a visitor.

My heart began racing, causing the monitors to go crazy, the doctor and nurses all came running in asking what's happening? I told them the story behind what was taking place and that I was not allowed to see or speak to anyone from the outside via court order.

That came with some relief, because now I felt safe and no longer to be harmed, no more running or hiding.

Right now; I also feel the need to say this. Too many of us, women has suffered many years from the abuse of the people in our lives that's supposed to love us, but yet hurt us. And yes; I'm still trying to figure out yet another one of life mysteries.

Many have lost and many will lose their lives, then there will be those as myself that carries the scars of the abuse for a life time. Our younger generations of girls, boys, teenagers, and young adults are becoming victims of this crime. All in the name of love.

Some of us can and will cover up the scars because of shame, but there are many women that walk around every day and their scars are on display for the world to see. What if this hits your doorsteps? Would you like it if no one reach out to help? or is it possible, that you can go on as if nothing is happening or has happened and you continue to go on just turn your head and go on with your life.

When you have been broken down and left to pick up the pieces alone, moving on is hard, and I kid you not; it's hard and many of us don't make it back. Many succumb to becoming drug addicts, some to alcoholism, some to prostitution, I swallowed a half bottled of Tylenol, not once, but twice, sure I came away and got it together, but look what it took for me to get out. I was willing to end my life because I as many others stay, because they are led to believe that there is no way out. "Another Lie from the Devil"

Just For Thoughts
We can stand as a Nation, but the strongest of nation is DETREMINATION"

I was so determined to pull myself away from those dark places in my life that I became desperate, and knew the only way out was to trust and depend on the love of God. I wanted to be free, not just in lip service, but I meant it from the very core of my being, and learning that in order for one to be free, my mindset had to change, and then search out a way for that freedom.

I did break free from the abuse because I later moved away, but the scars, they lingered until this day. Can you imagine what it's like to bear these scars for the rest of your life? Maybe you can, or maybe you can't if you or anyone for that matter have never experience it first hand.

For those of you that have been there and have suffered in silence, make a choice to live and take a stand against abuse. I have no remorse for any man/ woman that goes to jail or have had their lives interrupted because of their irrational thinking, and their insecurities, that causes their actions to harm others.

It took a long time for the laws to change concerning domestic violence/abuse, but it did; and I'm one that appreciate the men and women that fought for this law. I also tip my hat off to the many women that faught back and won.

> *"Fear thou not, for I am with thee: be not dismayed;*
> *for I am thy God: I will strengthen thee; yea I will*
> *help thee: yea, I will uphold thee with the right hand*
> *of my righteousness" (Isa 41:10)*

Now I can say I'm free and that means more to me than anything. I said early on, that in all I went through I still have my life. Yes; I messed up, time and time again, but I kept on pushing and fighting for that which God has given me, my life and my inheritance.

To make my point clear, don't allow the devil to tell you there is nothing that can't be done, or that you'll never survive after being pull through the mud and having to live life in the "pig-sty".

We know the story of the young man from the Bible that got all his riches, went to a far country, wasted it all on riotous living, later to find himself broken, homeless, n eating with the pigs. Well when he came to himself, he made up his mind and went home. There he found himself back in his father's arms and being welcome back. This is all I had to do. Get up, shake myself off, and get back to my father (Jesus) where I have everything I needed and all I long for. His love, which is unfailing and everlasting.

The devil's purpose is to steal, kill, and destroy, and if you don't fight back with the strength of the Lord you will be defeated. God gave His son to die so that we/I could have life, and that more abundantly, but if you/I give in to the lies the devil has told us or is telling us, we will die.

Maybe not the physical death, and unfortunately many will and many have, but to live and then die a spiritual death is the worst of all. Life without Christ, is a life without meaning and hope. But with Him you/I can live life to the fullest of our potential having all hope. And believing that He can and He will make a way when you can't see your way.

> *Just For Thoughts*
> *"You never know how strong you are, until being strong is the only choice you have"*

My Second Little Miracle

THE DELIVERY WAS quick, and fearful, there was difficulties, he was under weight (3lb-1oz), and his lungs had collapsed. Those nurses was moving so fast I didn't get to see him, they had to take him up to the Neo-natal clinic quickly to be cared for.

The doctors worked on me trying to stop the hemorraging while assuring me that the baby was in the hands of the best neo-natal care team they had to offer. I later went to sleep because I was so tired from all the excitement that went on that evening.

Two weeks had past, I was home recovering and wondering when I would be able to see my son. I called every day to keep up with his progress, and his nurse assured me that he was a fighter. He has gained 2lbs, breathing on his own and eating well.

Now that's the kind of God we serve when one is sincere about their deliverance and standard with Him, He will always come through and allow us to experience His grace.

The grandmother called and said she had stopped in to check on him (the baby) and the nurse allowed her to hold him. But this is what got to me, there was two other visitors there and when I was told who it was, I could have walked to that hospital and taken both their lives. But I held my peace.

> *"Do not be overcome by evil, but overcome evil with good"*
> *(Rom 12:21)*

Now when I think about how bad this could of went if I had of allowed (Jennifer) to do what she wanted to do, "But God" that is all I can say because It wasn't me, and for this I really appreciate (even in my madness) the guiding hands of God that gave me enough self-control to walk away.

Just to think of the goodness of Jesus and how He kept me through all those rough times and my deepest valleys, with all the insults that came from the people I called family and friends. All the discouragements, even in my brokenness, I can turly say "Thank You Jesus."

I often ask myself "why God allowed these terrible things to happen. When all I wanted was to be me, I wanted to be loved and cared for because I have so much to give. I wanted to be heard, but no one would listen. So I learned to laugh when everyone laugh at me.

I became one with myself and began living the life that was granted to me.

Now; I do believe I have done and yet doing exactly what I was meant to do. In spite of all my mistake, my down falls, my dirt, through the mud, the grit and grimes. I have been called for a time as this. He has kept me through it all, He is still keeping me, guiding, protecting, providing, and so much more. And for that I am a grateful woman.

Knowing that Jesus has all things in control gives me more of a reason to live and don't have to live in fear, because He did not give me a spirit of fear; but that of a sound mind and love that cast out all fear. He was with me then, and He's with me now, He has never left me alone and that is the goodness of it all.

Just For Thoughts
"I am so grateful for the difficult people in and out of my life; for they have shown me exactly who I don't want to be"

Seeing Others Through The Eyes Of God

A FTER ALL THE drama I really had to sit and search myself for answers because I understood me, but I could not understand the others that had entered into my life, and what I did to deserved such actions toward me.

When I/we seek God for answers sometimes I/we will not understnd His ways or His answers, but whatever, and however it comes, trust me; it is for my/our good and our growth, not only in the natural, but it is more for my/our spiritual growth.

Then one day I came across this article in a Daily Devotion booklet which was a discussion between the Pastor and one of his followers whom had been in an abusive relationship. Now I had to read this article because I wanted to learn how that Pastor responded to the question where I found myself also. It read as followed; how would you respond to the news that the very person(s) that sought to harm you has been hurt or even killed? How Ironic, but I was true in my answers and to my feelings at that time in my life because I was still so angry, and hurt and I answered within myself how any other person would, bitter and angry.

This was a battle, because as a person with personality disorder *was torn between me as myself, and the other side of who I had allowed to be a part of me. Then having to make a choice to continue in my anger, and unforgivness or to forgive and ask God to help me to overcome it.*

The Jennifer in me wanted to laugh and say so what, it's deserving. I was really enjoying my freedom of speech but when I finished reading I was disappointed in how I felt, but I was real. That part of me did not want to do what I knew was right, so instead of taking that time to begun my healing and choose to forgive, I choice what I felt good to my flesh.

Three month after I read this article, I got word that this very thing happened to someone that once caused me such grief, and the words that came out of mouth was "Good, I wished it was death" and in that instance, that voice inside convicted me. Oh yeah, somehow it seems as if the very thing we pray about, becomes our test.

Did I apologized for what was said? No not at first, but after a week or so I did, and I asked God for forgivness, then I had to ask myself "was this a sign of weakness? I had no idea how I was to respond to this, and really thought this through, and decided it wasn't.

It was then that I knew I was beginning to conform into what God was doing on the inside and that I was learning to look past the indiviual(s) that was the source of my pain and consider how God would look at me if this was reversed.

Just for Thoughts
"Because of the Lord's great love we are not consumed, for His compassions never fail. They are new every morning; great is your faithfulness. (Lam 3: 22-23)

*A*s I looked deep into my real self, I saw my flaws, my lies, my mistake, and the many times God had forgiven me, and knew that when He looks at me He saw that I needed help to learn how to deal with all of my hurt and pain. Than it hit me like a ton of bricks, that through His pain and suffering (Jesus) was able to give His life for me/us, He looks beyond His accuser's faults and saw their great needs, and not what was happening or or what has been done to Him.

Wow; what a revelation. When I began to see myself in Jesus shoes, by taking my focus off of what was done to me rather then who did it I was able to really understand the article and what the Pastor was saying.

In the conclusion to the article the Pastor stated "we are not to retaliate, but we must seek Him through prayer and get the full understanding behind one's actions". Now I know and believe that this is His way of bringing us to a level of grace we never thought was possible. Truly (His grace is sufficient). And believing that to be truth was good enough for me.

Again; I remembered reading a couple years ago, (and I thank God I love to read) about our many afflictions and how God uses them to make us fruitful, so I took this into consideration not just for that moment but trying to live it for a life time, knowing that the bible has answers to any questions I/we may have. But we must get into His Words and walk it out in faith and not by my/our own thoughts and beliefs.

Just For Thoughts
"In the moments of our afflictions, and through our battles, it's the place where God will make us fruitful"

Something else about that article made me more aware of the way I wanted to live when I came across this statement; "He will make us fruitful in a way that our hearts will be fully satisfied; and His heart fully glorified." Who wouldn't want this in their lives? This is what has/is helping me every day in my walk. Just the thought of knowing that I/we can be fruitful even when I/we have so many issues.

While sitting there thinking about what I had just read these words were spoken into my spirit concerning all the bitterness I had kept inside, not realizing I was doing nothing but to hurt myself and that I was/had been contaminating my heart and mind, and that He (God) couldn't do what was/is needed so I could be used for His Glory.

Not sure who wrote this, but as I said before, when I come across articles that are or can be useful to my growth, I take it in and use it to began the transformation of my way of thinking and stop trying to analyze everything. This was something else that caught my attention quickly.

It stated that; when I/we harbor the bitterness, it grows until it eventually defiles us and others around us. Now I'm thinking, how is this possible when I'm not the one causing the hurt, I didn't cause anyone any pain, but it wasn't the action taken, but just the thought of it was just as bad. Knowing that if I had allowed all that bitterness to take root for all the hurt and pain sustained from the hands and mouth of others, I would have become imprisoned even more then I already was, and the grace of God would have no effect in my life. Now that is/was sad.

So choosing to forgive, (not to forget) I became somewhat free to live in God's supernatural grace, because with His grace comes freedom, a freedom that will teach us how to love and accept the person (s) that have been the source of my/our pain.

In this freedom I am in a place where God's power is most revealed, so I began working on how to change my mindset so I could really be free. I knew I was changing slowly because I was beginning to not feel so much anger, but I also knew I was still hiding behind those mask being cautious so I could protect myself.

Delayed Is Not Always Denial

AGAIN; AS I find myself on this journey, I must understand that because God have not answered a prayer doesn't mean He won't. It is only put on hold to build my/our faith, patience, trust, and my/our strength. This was a sermon preached about ten years ago, not knowing I would be using the nuggets that stayed in my heart and spirit. Trusting God when things we ask are delayed is never easy but I've learned that His delays are necessary. God sometimes must delay His work in us/me to accomplished what is needed for His purpose. As people of God, my/our stages are already set so that what is to be accomplished for His glory and not mine/ours, is revealed through the events that has been orchestrated by Him and Him alone.

Many years I struggled with what was placed in my spirit. I knew at the age of fifteen I was called to a place of greater works but didn't understand what it all meant, and that became my fight. (Flesh-vs-Spirit. His delays, and the many unfulfilling path I took, was and still is being prepared for me for the greatest of glory that He is to receive. I/we have/must learn to live with patience and not become unraveled when we are put in a holding pattern.

I must believe and know, that God is at work because He knows the purpose for my/our delays, and if I/we don't become faint or weary in my/our delays, it will demonsrate His greatest glory, but I/we must remain faithful through it all. (firey trails)

I will give you a new heart and put a new spirit in you; I will remove from you your heart of stone and give you a heart of flesh. (Ezel 36:26)

The first twenty-three years of my life has had a lot of bumps and bruises, many tears, and a whole lot of pain. A childhood of memories that I love to share, a father that stole my heart with his humor, his hugs, and his laughter, those that my sisters and brothers didn't have a chance to enjoy because of different circumstances.

A mother that was a lioness protecting her own the best she knew, with her sternness, her eyes, and most of all her words that cut to the bones. Memories that I could go on and on about and being grateful for. But the best of memories, is learning how to trust and depend on the Lord in all things and being thankful for the good and the bad for in it all is where we found our most strenght.

To be robbed of my childhood by someone with no conscience, to being taunted by others because of the color of my hair, which is far better than being judge by the color of my skin, then being ripped away from a place of familiarity to having to learn how to start over again.

Then just when I thought all was well; my hero dies leaving me in a place of brokenness, alcholism, abuse, to creating two other personalities for safety, while almost losing myself in the dysfunction, and then; living a life of shame of who I had become.

Falling in love with the idea of being in love, and the lust of it all. Left to carry the burdens on my own, struggling to keep food on the table, clothes on our backs and making sure we never feeling any kind of abandoment.

Thinking all those that took part in their lives, to the one that wanted to take full control of the Who, What, When, Where, and Why, of our lives and leaving me with no alternative but to do what I knew best.

So when God blessed me with His precious gift of having children, they became my obsession. To love them and care for them was my only motive, nothing less than that, but to give them the only thing I had (My Love).

God gave me is best and I tried to give them my best, and many times I failed, I messed up, I just did what I thought was best and in doing that I made many mistakes, some I regret while others taught me meaningful lessons f life.

The broken heart, and spirit, I was left with, has taught me how to love deeper and harder, to laugh louder and even alone, and to live life like today is my last, knowing no one could take that away.

And the thing that taught me the most; was how I've learned through it all to trust in God even more, believe in who I am, and knowing that I can do whatever I wanted to do if I just keep my mind in a place of peace.

There is nothing so valuable in life than peace and I refuse to let anyone, or anything steal that from me again. God has given me a peace that is unexplainable, but extraordinary, and this is "MY" peace that the cares of this world will never interrupt again.

Just For Thoughts
God has not promise to keep us from the valley of suffering, but to make us fruitful in them.

Habits, weather good or bad; can become habitual and very dangerous if the actions are not brought attention to. Society has allowed so many bad habits to infiltrate our homes, schools, communities, etc.... that it's become the norm.

What we hear and see plays a big part in our growth from childhood to adulthood, and when these actions, and habits are allowed to continue for the purpose of breaking another person's image or character without confronting it, it causes much damage, (prime example) and that for me was where I'm learning to draw the line when it comes to knowing who I am, and hope to be, where I'm going, to where I've been, and what I will allow myself to believe about me.

Just for Thoughts
How assuring to know that when we hold our peace, even when being tempted to speak angrily to hurt those that have hurt or harm us, one must select to choose love over hate, and face the truth over our error.

Printed in the United States
By Bookmasters